To the Nature Lover and Mineral Collector

You may have had the experience of looking at an especially pretty stone while on a walk, or perhaps you found a sparkling rock crystal while hiking in the mountains. You may wish to learn more about these minerals—where they are found and how to differentiate one mineral from another. Or you may be a mineral collector and want to know which minerals to acquire for your collection.

This new guide to minerals introduces you to the fascinating world of minerals and crystals. It shows the most important and most common minerals in their familiar forms. With the help of brilliant color photographs you will learn to recognize the most important minerals. The short descriptive text and the color key make identification easy.

This mineral guide is the ideal companion for nature walks. It fits into a jacket or pants pocket, has a durable cover, and is lightweight. It will help you to discover a wealth of form and color you may never have been aware of before. If you are buying minerals, this little book will be invaluable to you.

The author and the editors wish you much pleasure in collecting and identifying minerals.

S0-BZW-824

Identification of Minerals

In this guide to minerals the most common and most important minerals are presented in order of increasing hardness. Color photographs of specially selected mineral specimens show each mineral in its most common and typical form. Concise descriptions give details about crystal form, place of origin, accompanying minerals, and properties that distinguish them from other, similar minerals. Thus identification is made easy even for the novice.

Front cover: agate (*interior*) with **amethyst** (*exterior*).
Back cover: quartz (amethyst) (*top left*), **beryl** (*top right*),
fluorite (*bottom left* and *right*).

Explanation of the Descriptions

The name of the mineral appears above each photograph. The caption provides the source of the specimen and the magnification used. Brief, general information about the mineral introduces the text. Concise comments follow on **Color** and *luster*. (Words used to describe luster include *metallic*; *adamantine*—brilliant, almost metallic; *vitreous*—glassy; *greasy*; *resinous*; and *pearly*.) **Cleavage** and *fracture* describe the way the mineral tends to break when struck. (*Conchoidal* fracture is a curving, glasslike break.) **Crystal Form** provides both crystal system (*cubic*, *hexagonal*, etc.) and growth habit (*reniform*, *acicular*, etc.; see inside front cover). Next, details are given on **Where Found** and what minerals the particular substance is usually **Found With. Hardness** is given on the Mohs scale (which ranges from talc—the softest mineral, graded 1; to diamond—the hardest, at 10). Finally, *Specific Gravity* (a measure of density obtained by comparing the weight of a substance with the weight of an equal volume of water), *Streak Color* (see below), and *Chemical Formula* are given. The distinguishing characteristics of other minerals with which the mineral may be confused are presented under the heading **Similar Minerals.**

Explanation of the Color Key

The streak color of the mineral described can be seen at once by glancing at the colored bar that borders the illustration. (Streak is best demonstrated by rubbing the specimen in question across the surface of an unglazed ceramic tile.)

Minerals with a white or very pale streak

Minerals with a bright blue to blue-green streak

Minerals with a pink to red-brown streak

Minerals with a bright yellow or orange to ochre streak

Minerals with a yellow-brown to red-brown streak

Minerals with a bright green, blue-green, or gray-green to black-green streak

Minerals with a gray to black streak

Graphite

Namibia 10X

Graphite is a very important mineral economically. Since it produces a gray streak on paper, it is used, among other things, for making pencils.

Color: Dark to light steel gray. Metallic luster to dull.
Cleavage: Perfect.
Crystal Form: Hexagonal. Well-developed crystals are rare; usually thin plates or leaves, scaly, massive.
Where Found: In metamorphic limestones and schists; sometimes in pegmatites.

Found with: Diopside, wollastonite, calcite.
Hardness: 1
Specific Gravity: 2.1–2.3
Streak Color: Black
Chemical Formula: C
Similar Minerals: Molybdenite is somewhat harder; its streak is greenish when rubbed with the corner of a second streak tablet.

Korea 2X

Molybdenite is the most important molybdenum ore. Artificially produced molybdenite is used as a lubricant. When the streak is rubbed with the corner of a second streak tablet, it shows a dirty green color.

Color: Blue-gray. Metallic luster.
Cleavage: Perfect. Individual sheets bend very easily.
Crystal Form: Hexagonal. Tabular crystals, scaly sheets.
Where Found: In pegmatites and quartz veins.

Found with: Quartz, pyrite.
Hardness: 1
Specific Gravity: 4.8
Streak Color: Dark gray.
Chemical Formula: MoS_2
Similar Minerals: The rubbed streak of graphite is more metallic and not greenish.

Italy 2X

Sulfur occurs in nature as beautiful, well-formed crystals. The transparent crystals become cloudy in the warm hand and crack.

Color: Yellow. Resinous to greasy luster; adamantine luster on crystal faces.
Cleavage: None. Conchoidal fracture. Very brittle.
Crystal Form: Orthorhombic. Bipyramidal, fibrous, powdery, massive.
Where Found: In places where volcanic gases have escaped; in oxidation zones; in sediments.
Found with: Gypsum, calcite, aragonite, sulfide minerals.
Hardness: 2
Specific Gravity: 2.0–2.1
Streak Color: White
Chemical Formula: α-S
Similar Minerals: Sphalerite is easily distinguished from sulfur by its good cleavage.

California, USA 1X

Rock salt, which in its most common form is used as table salt, occurs in large deposits exploited as salt mines. Rock salt is soluble in water.

Color: Colorless, red, yellow, gray, blue. Vitreous luster.
Cleavage: Easy, cubic. Conchoidal fracture.
Crystal Form: Cubic. Almost exclusively cubes, sometimes also octahedrons, often massive.
Where Found: Forms rock salt deposits in limestones, clays, marls.
Found with: Gypsum, anhydrite, carnallite, sylvite.
Hardness: 2
Specific Gravity: 2.1–2.22
Streak Color: White
Chemical Formula: NaCl
Similar Minerals: Fluorite is harder and not water-soluble.

Gypsum is a very common mineral that often forms rock masses. It is used in the building industry.

Alberta, Canada 1X (*top*)
West Germany, 3X (*bottom*)

Color: Colorless, white. Pearly luster.
Cleavage: Easy. Conchoidal fracture.
Crystal Form: Monoclinic. Prismatic, acicular, tabular, often twinned with "swallowtail" corners (see photo at bottom), fibrous, massive.
Where Found: Forms rock masses, crystals in clay; occurs in ore veins.
Found with: Anhydrite, rock salt.
Hardness: 2
Specific Gravity: 2.3–2.4
Streak Color: White.
Chemical Formula: $CaSO_4 \cdot 2H_2O$
Similar Minerals: Cleavage and low hardness distinguish gypsum from all other minerals.

Micas are a group of minerals notable for their tabular crystals and extraordinarily flaky cleavage. The most common mica is the light-colored *muscovite* (see photo at left), with the chemical formula $KAl_3Si_3O_{10}(OH)_2$. In other micas potassium and aluminum are replaced by different minerals: iron and magnesium (*biotite*, photo at top right), lithium (*lepidolite*, photo on page 9), magnesium (*phlogopite*, photo at bottom right), or lithium and iron (*zinnwaldite*).

Switzerland 2X (*left*)
Madagascar 3X (*top right*)
Switzerland 20X (*bottom right*)

Color: Silver gray to greenish (muscovite, zinnwaldite), pink to lavender (lepidolite), black to brown (biotite, phlogopite). Pearly luster.
Cleavage: Extraordinarily easy.
Crystal Form: Monoclinic. Six-sided plates, sheets, scales, rosettes.

California, USA 2X

Where Found: Micas are important components of almost all rocks. Muscovite is found in granites and gneisses and is the major component of mica schists. Biotite is found in granites and volcanic rocks. Phlogopite often occurs in metamorphic rocks. Zinnwaldite and lepidolite are found in pegmatites and pneumatolytic deposits.

Found with: Quartz, feldspar.

Hardness: 2–3
Specific Gravity: 2.8–3.2
Streak Color: White.
Similar Minerals: Talc is softer. The flaky cleavage and the flexibility of individual sheets distinguish micas from all other minerals.

Mercury, the only liquid metal, is obtained from cinnabar.

Austria 6X

Color: Bright red to brown-red. Adamantine luster.
Cleavage: Easy. Splintery fracture (subconchoidal).
Crystal Form: Trigonal. Sometimes forms thick tabular crystals; usually massive and as crust.
Where Found: Pure cinnabar deposits; as weathering product of ores containing small amounts of mercury.
Found with: Pyrite, calcite, chalcedony, quartz.
Hardness: 2–2½
Specific Gravity: 8.1
Streak Color: Red.
Chemical Formula: HgS
Similar Minerals: Red sphalerite is much lighter, harder, and has a different cleavage. Red hematite and rutile are much harder. Cuprite can be distinguished by the hydrochloric acid test.

Michigan, USA 3X

Native copper is found as beautiful crystals and aggregates weighing up to several hundred pounds. It is not important as a copper ore. On the surface it is often mixed with malachite.

Color: Copper red to dark red. Metallic luster.
Cleavage: None. Jagged fracture. Malleable and ductile.
Crystal Form: Cubic. Cubes, octahedrons, usually strongly deformed; skeletal shapes, corrugated and filiform; massive.

Where Found: In copper deposits at the boundary between secondary enrichment and oxidation zones.
Found with: Cuprite, calcite, malachite, azurite.
Hardness: 2½–3
Specific Gravity: 8.93
Streak Color: Copper red, metallic.
Chemical Formula: Cu

Native silver was once an important silver ore. Today silver is recovered mainly from other minerals. It can be cut and beaten into plates.

West Germany 2X

Color: Silver white but often yellowish or blackish. Metallic luster.
Cleavage: None. Jagged fracture. Malleable.
Crystal Form: Cubic. Distorted cubes, skeletal, corrugated and filiform, massive.
Where Found: In the conversion zones of silver-containing deposits.
Found with: Argentite, proustite, galena.
Hardness: 2½–3
Specific Gravity: 9.6–12
Streak Color: White, metallic.
Chemical Formula: Ag
Similar Minerals: Galena and other silver-gray minerals cannot be cut.

Galena

Almost all the lead used in industry is obtained from galena.

West Germany 3X

Color: Lead gray. Strong metallic luster, often running to dull or blue.
Cleavage: Very easy along cubic planes.
Crystal Form: Cubic. Often massive, otherwise cubes alone or combined with octahedrons; occasionally octahedrons only.
Where Found: Principally in metallic ore veins.
Found with: Sphalerite, chalcopyrite, pyrite, calcite, barite, and fluorite.
Hardness: 2½–3
Specific Gravity: 7.2–7.6
Streak Color: Gray-black.
Chemical Formula: PbS
Similar Minerals: With its color, luster, and cleavage, galena can scarcely be confused with other minerals.

Tasmania 6X

Crocoite is rare and occurs only where lead ores and chromium minerals have weathered at the same time. Because of its beautiful red crystals, it is prized by mineral collectors.

Color: Red with occasional tints of yellow. Greasy to adamantine luster.
Cleavage: Scarcely perceptible. Conchoidal fracture.
Crystal Form: Monoclinic. Acicular to prismatic crystals, massive.
Where Found: In the oxidation zone of lead deposits.
Found with: Cerussite, pyromorphite.
Hardness: 2½–3
Specific Gravity: 5.9–6
Streak Color: Orange.
Chemical Formula: $Pb[CrO_4]$
Similar Minerals: Cinnabar is almost never prismatic. Cuprite effervesces in contact with a drop of hydrochloric acid.

Gold occurs in nature as crystals, flakes, or nuggets. It can be cut and beaten into plates.

California, USA 6X (left)
Colombia 3X (top right)
California, USA 2X (bottom right)

Color: Golden to brass yellow. Metallic luster.

Cleavage: None. Jagged fracture. Very malleable.

Crystal Form: Cubic. Octahedrons, cubes, skeleton shapes, corrugated and filiform.

Where Found: In hydrothermal veins of gold-bearing ores, alluvial deposits (placers).

Found with: Quartz, arsenopyrite, pyrite, tourmaline.

Hardness: 2½–3

Specific Gravity: 15.5–19.3

Streak Color: Golden yellow, metallic.

Chemical Formula: Au

Similar Minerals: Chalcopyrite, pyrite, and marcasite cannot be cut and have different streak colors.

Morocco 5X

The valuable metal vanadium is obtained from vanadinite. Vanadinite is popular with collectors because of its beautiful red color.

Color: Yellow, brown, orange, red. Adamantine luster, somewhat greasy.
Cleavage: None. Conchoidal fracture.
Crystal Form: Hexagonal. Six-sided prisms and plates.
Where Found: In oxidation zones.
Found with: Wulfenite, pyromorphite, mimetite.
Hardness: 3
Specific Gravity: 6.8–7.1
Streak Color: White, yellowish.
Chemical Formula: $Pb_5[Cl/(VO_4)_3]$
Similar Minerals: Red-colored vanadinite is unmistakable; other colors are not distinguishable from mimetite and pyromorphite by simple means.

England 6X

Olivenite is a typical mineral occurring in the oxidation zone of copper deposits. It often forms very beautiful crystals.

Color: Bright to olive green. Vitreous luster.
Cleavage: None. Conchoidal fracture.
Crystal Form: Orthorhombic. Tabular to prismatic crystals. Acicular, hairlike, radiated aggregate.
Where Found: In the oxidation zone of copper deposits.
Found with: Azurite, mala-chite, adamite.
Hardness: 3
Specific Gravity: 4.3
Streak Color: Yellow to olive green.
Chemical Formula: $Cu_2[OH/ASO_4]$
Similar Minerals: Malachite is closer to emerald green. Copper adamite usually is much lighter and not acicular.

Calcite

Calcite is one of the most widely distributed minerals. Many familiar rocks, such as limestones or marbles, consist almost entirely of calcite. Calcite effervesces with dilute hydrochloric acid.

West Germany 0.5X (top left)
West Germany 2X (bottom left)
West Germany 1X (right)

Color: Colorless, white, various colors. Vitreous luster.
Cleavage: Very easy. Conchoidal fracture.
Crystal Form: Trigonal. Rhombohedral, scalenohedral; often massive.
Where Found: Practically everywhere.
Found with: Dolomite, quartz, metallic ores.
Hardness: 3
Specific Gravity: 2.6–2.8
Streak Color: White.
Chemical Formula: $CaCO_3$
Similar Minerals: Quartz is harder. Dolomite effervesces only with hot hydrochloric acid. Gypsum is softer.

Austria 6X

This mineral is found in the oxidation zone of lead ores.

Color: Yellow to orange-red. Adamantine to resinous luster.
Cleavage: Pyramidal. Conchoidal fracture. Brittle.
Crystal Form: Tetragonal. Acute bipyramidal; thick to thin tablets.
Where Found: Oxidation product of lead ores.
Found with: Cerussite, pyromorphite, mimetite, hemimorphite, hydrozincite.
Hardness: 3

Specific Gravity: 6.7–6.9
Streak Color: White.
Chemical Formula: $PbMoO_4$
Similar Minerals: Appearance and occurrence with other lead and zinc oxidation minerals make confusion impossible.

Barite

Morocco 2X

The outstanding characteristic of barite is its specific gravity. It is much heavier than similar minerals.

Color: Colorless, white, yellow, blue. Pearly luster.
Cleavage: Easy. Conchoidal fracture.
Crystal Form: Orthorhombic. Tabular crystals, sawtoothed; in sand occurs as flower-shaped aggregates; often massive.
Where Found: In hydrothermal veins, sedimentary deposits.

Found with: Calcite, quartz, fluorite, metallic ores.
Hardness: 3–3½
Specific Gravity: 4.48
Streak Color: White.
Chemical Formula: $BaSO_4$
Similar Minerals: Quartz and feldspar are harder; gypsum, calcite, and aragonite are much lighter.

Adamite occurs in the oxidation zone of zinc ore deposits. Pure adamite is colorless to yellow; the presence of added metals produces green *copper adamite* and pink to lavendar *cobalt adamite*.

Namibia 2X (*top left*)
Mexico 2X (*bottom left*)
Mexico 5X (*right*)

Color: Colorless, white, yellow, green, lavender. Vitreous luster.
Cleavage: Scarcely perceptible. Conchoidal fracture.
Crystal Form: Orthorhombic. Prismatic to acicular, radiated.
Where Found: In the oxidation zone.
Found with: Smithsonite, olivenite.
Hardness: 3½
Specific Gravity: 4.3–4.5
Streak Color: White.
Chemical Formula: $Zn[OH/AsO_4]$
Similar Minerals: Olivenite is almost always clearly yellow-green.

West Germany 10X

Tetrahedrite is an important copper ore in which, depending on the location, either arsenic (tennantite) or antimony (tetrahedrite) predominate.

Color: Steel gray to iron black. Metallic luster, but also frequently dull.
Cleavage: Practically none. Conchoidal fracture. Brittle.
Crystal Form: Cubic. Usually only tetrahedral, sometimes polyhedral to globular (binnite), often massive.
Where Found: Chiefly in hydrothermal veins.
Found with: Pyrite, sphalerite, chalcopyrite.
Hardness: 3–4
Specific Gravity: 4.6–5.2
Streak Color: Black.
Chemical Formula: $Cu_3(As,Sb)S_{3.25}$
Similar Minerals: Galena has easy cleavage. Graphite is softer.

Sweden 4X

Strengite is an alteration product of phosphate deposits and often forms particularly beautiful crystals.

Color: Colorless, white, yellow, pink, lavender. Vitreous luster.
Cleavage: Basal perfect. Conchoidal fracture.
Crystal Form: Orthorhombic. Tabular crystals. Radiated, globular, reniform aggregates, scales, crusts.
Where Found: In iron deposits, phosphate-bearing pegmatites.
Found with: Rockbridgeite, goethite, beraunite.
Hardness: 3–4
Specific Gravity: 2.87
Streak Color: White.
Chemical Formula: $Fe(PO_4)\% 2H_2O$
Similar Minerals: Amethyst is much harder.

West Germany 5X

The deep blue azurite is a particularly beautiful alteration product of copper ores. It effervesces when touched by a drop of dilute hydrochloric acid.

Color: Deep blue; somewhat lighter in massive form. Vitreous luster.

Cleavage: Perfect. Conchoidal fracture.

Crystal Form: Monoclinic. Columnar to tabular crystals, crusts; earthy.

Where Found: In the oxidation zone of copper-bearing deposits.

Found with: Limonite, malachite.

Hardness: 3½–4

Specific Gravity: 3.7–3.9

Streak Color: Blue.

Chemical Formula: $Cu_3[OH/CO_3]_2$

Similar Minerals: Its color, the hydrochloric acid test, and its occurrence in copper-bearing deposits differentiate azurite from practically all other minerals.

Arizona, USA 6X

Cuprite is a mineral that often appears in the oxidation zone of copper ores and is very noticeable because of its red color. It effervesces in the presence of hydrochloric acid.

Color: Deep red to brown-red. Metallic luster; often dull in aggregate form.
Cleavage: Poor. Conchoidal fracture.
Crystal Form: Cubic. Octahedrons, sometimes cubes. Hairlike, granular, massive.
Where Found: In the oxidation zone of copper deposits.
Found with: Native copper, limonite, malachite.
Hardness: 3½–4
Specific Gravity: 6.15
Streak Color: Brown-red.
Chemical Formula: Cu_2O
Similar Minerals: Cinnabar and hematite do not effervesce with hydrochloric acid. Hematite is much harder.

West Germany 6X

Dolomite is an important mineral that forms rocks and mountains (for example, the Dolomites). It effervesces only with heated hydrochloric acid.

Color: Colorless, white, brownish, blackish, gray. Vitreous luster.
Cleavage: Into perfect rhombohedrons. Conchoidal fracture.
Crystal Form: Trigonal. Rhombohedral crystals, often massive.
Where Found: In rock formations; also in metallic ore veins.
Found with: Quartz, calcite, and many other minerals.
Hardness: 3½–4
Specific Gravity: 2.85–2.95
Streak Color: White.
Chemical Formula: $CaMg(CO_3)_2$
Similar Minerals: Calcite effervesces with dilute hydrochloric acid.

West Germany 2X

Golden yellow chalcopyrite is one of the most important copper ores. Emerald green malachite often develops when it weathers.

Color: Brass yellow with greenish tint; often iridescent. Metallic luster.
Cleavage: Scarcely noticeable. Conchoidal fracture.
Crystal Form: Tetragonal. Tetrahedronlike or octahedronlike crystals, often massive.
Where Found: In metallic ore deposits.

Found with: Pyrite, sphalerite, tetrahedrite, pyrrhotite, calcite, barite, dolomite, quartz.
Hardness: 3½–4
Specific Gravity: 4.2–4.3
Streak Color: Greenish black.
Chemical Formula: $CuFeS_2$
Similar Minerals: Pyrite is harder. Pyrrhotite is browner in color. Gold is softer and can be cut.

Pyromorphite

Pyromorphite can occur in various colors. It is also known as green lead ore.

Australia 4X (*top left*)
England 2X (*top right*)
West Germany 3X (*bottom*)

Color: Green, brown, orange to colorless. Greasy luster.
Cleavage: None. Conchoidal fracture.
Crystal Form: Hexagonal. Prisms, barrel-like forms, crusts.
Where Found: Oxidation product of lead minerals.
Found with: Wulfenite, galena, cerussite.
Hardness: 3½–4
Specific Gravity: 6.7–7

Streak Color: White.
Chemical Formula: $Pb_5[Cl/(PO_4)_3]$
Similar Minerals: Apatite and quartz are harder.

Yugoslavia 5X

Sphalerite occurs in many colors. It is the most important zinc ore.

Color: Bright yellow to brown to black, red, green. Nearly adamantine luster.
Cleavage: Perfect along dodecahedral planes.
Crystal Form: Cubic. Tetrahedral, often octahedral, tabular twins; often massive.
Where Found: In tin and zinc ore deposits.
Found with: Galena, pyrrhotite, pyrite, calcite.

Hardness: 3½–4
Specific Gravity: 3.9–4.2
Streak Color: Shades of light brown.
Chemical Formula: ZnS
Similar Minerals: Differentiated from galena, tetrahedrite, and sulfur by hardness and cleavage.

Fluorite

Fluorite, with its beautiful, sparkling, varicolored crystals, is especially coveted by mineral collectors.

Switzerland 0.5X *(top left)*
Austria 1X *(top right)*
Spain 2X *(bottom left)*
West Germany 2X *(bottom right)*

Color: Colorless, pink, yellow, brown, green, blue, violet. Vitreous luster.
Cleavage: Perfect, octahedral.
Crystal Form: Cubic. Most common are cubes and octahedrons; often massive.
Where Found: In fluorite veins in Alpine fissures.
Found with: Barite, calcite.

Hardness: 4
Specific Gravity: 3.1–3.2
Streak Color: White.
Chemical Formula: CaF_2
Similar Minerals: Rock salt is water-soluble and much softer.

Wavellite is a mineral that often forms particularly beautiful stellated aggregates in rock fissures.

England 3X

Color: Colorless, white, yellow, green. Vitreous luster.
Cleavage: Not perceptible. Uneven fracture.
Crystal Form: Orthorhombic. Acicular crystals; radiated, globular aggregates, stellated rosettes.
Where Found: In fissures of schists, in fractured granites, limestones, limonite deposits.

Found with: Strengite, cacoxenite.
Hardness: 4
Specific Gravity: 2.3–2.4
Streak Color: White.
Chemical Formula: $Al_3[(OH)_3/(PO_4)_2]\cdot 5H_2O$
Similar Minerals: Calcite and aragonite effervesce in the presence of hydrochloric acid.

Malachite

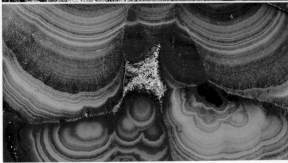

Malachite is a typical oxidation product of copper ores. The mineral effervesces immediately when brought into contact with dilute hydrochloric acid.

West Germany 4X (top)
Zaire 1.5X (bottom)

Color: Emerald green. Vitreous luster; silky in aggregates.
Cleavage: Not perceptible because of the crystal form. Conchoidal fracture.
Crystal Form: Monoclinic. Acicular clusters, hairlike aggregates, reniform crusts.
Where Found: Common oxidation product in copper-bearing deposits.
Found with: Limonite, azurite.
Hardness: 4
Specific Gravity: 4.0
Streak Color: Green.
Chemical Formula: $Cu_2[(OH)_2/CO_3]$
Similar Minerals: All similar minerals are much rarer.

Mexico 10X

Rhodochrosite is a prized stone for jewelry; because of its color, it is also called raspberry spar. The mineral effervesces only with hot hydrochloric acid.

Color: Pink to bright red. Vitreous luster.
Cleavage: Perfect. Uneven fracture.
Crystal Form: Trigonal. Rhombohedral, scalenohedral, radiated aggregates; often massive.
Where Found: In hydrothermal veins; occasionally in the oxidation zone of manganese ore deposits.
Found with: Quartz, rhodonite, limonite.
Hardness: 4
Specific Gravity: 3.3–3.6
Streak Color: White.
Chemical Formula: $MnCO_3$
Similar Minerals: Calcite effervesces even with dilute hydrochloric acid.

Kyanite/Disthene

Kyanite displays a characteristic that cannot be observed in any other mineral: it can be scratched with a steel needle in a longitudinal direction but not crosswise.

Switzerland 2X

Color: Blue, gray, whitish. Vitreous luster.
Cleavage: Perfect. Uneven fracture.
Crystal Form: Triclinic. Long, tabular to radiated crystals, always embedded in a rock groundmass.
Where Found: In metamorphic rocks.
Found with: Mica, staurolite.
Hardness: Lengthwise, 4–4½; across, 6–7
Specific Gravity: 3.6–3.7
Streak Color: White.
Chemical Formula: $Al_2[O/SiO_4]$
Similar Minerals: The directional difference in hardness distinguishes Kyanite from all other minerals.

Austria 1.5X

Siderite is an important iron ore. It effervesces only with hot hydrochloric acid.

Color: Yellow-white, yellow to dark-brown. Vitreous luster.
Cleavage: Perfect. Sparry fracture.
Crystal Form: Trigonal. Rhombohedral crystals, often bent into saddle shape; scalenohedral, often massive.
Where Found: In pegmatites, hydrothermal veins, sedimentary formations, in vesicles left by escaped gases in volcanic rocks.
Found with: Chalcedony, barite, calcite, metallic ore minerals.
Hardness: $4-4\frac{1}{2}$
Specific Gravity: 3.7–3.9
Streak Color: White.
Chemical Formula: $FeCO_3$
Similar Minerals: Calcite effervesces even with dilute hydrochloric acid. Sphalerite has a different cleavage.

West Germany 2X

As brown, earthy limonite, goethite is one of the commonest minerals in iron ore deposits; beautifully formed crystals are much rarer.

Color: Light yellow, brown to black-brown. Metallic to dull luster.
Cleavage: Perfect but not often perceptible. Uneven fracture.
Crystal Form: Orthorhombic. Acicular crystals, radiated aggregates with smooth surface areas, massive, earthy.

Where Found: Oxidation product of iron minerals.
Found with: Occurs with many different minerals.
Hardness: 5
Specific Gravity: 4.3
Streak Color: Brown.
Chemical Formula: FeOOH
Similar Minerals: Cannot be confused with other minerals.

West Germany 8X

Apatite is noteworthy because of its special variety of form and color. Thus it can easily be confused with many other minerals.

Color: Colorless, yellow, blue, green, violet, red. Vitreous luster.

Cleavage: Basal, sometimes well-developed. Conchoidal fracture.

Crystal Form: Hexagonal. Long prismatic to short prismatic, occasionally globular, acicular, also massive.

Where Found: In igneous rocks and pegmatites.

Found with: Magnetite, anatase, brookite, rutile, quartz, feldspar.

Hardness: 5

Specific Gravity: 3.16–3.22

Streak Color: White.

Chemical Formula: $Ca_5[(F,Cl)/(PO_4)_3]$

Similar Minerals: Quartz and beryl are harder. Calcite and pyromorphite are softer.

Austria 10X

Titanite is commonly found in many rocks as small, embedded crystals. Large crystals protruding from fractures in the Alps, called sphene, are especially prized by collectors.

Color: Colorless, yellow, greenish, red, brown, black-brown. Resinous luster.
Cleavage: Discernible. Conchoidal fracture.
Crystal Form: Monoclinic. Prismatic to tabular. Often crossed twins.
Where Found: In marbles and pegmatites, in Alpine fissures.
Found with: Anatase, rutile, brookite, quartz.
Hardness: 5–5½
Specific Gravity: 3.4–3.6
Streak Color: White.
Chemical Formula: $CaTi[O/SiO_4]$
Similar Minerals: Anatase is clearly tetragonal.

Hornblende is the name of a group of minerals whose common feature is a cleavage angle of 120 degrees.

Austria 0.5X (*left*)
West Germany 3X (*right*)

Color: Dark green, black. Vitreous luster.
Cleavage: Perfect. The cleavage planes form an angle of approximately 120 degrees. Uneven fracture.
Crystal Form: Monoclinic. Prismatic crystals, elongated and radiated, massive.
Where Found: In igneous, volcanic, and metamorphic rocks.
Found with: Biotite, augite, magnetite.
Hardness: 5–6
Specific Gravity: 2.9–3.4
Streak Color: Brown to greenish gray.
Chemical Formula: $(Ca,Na)_2 (Mg,Fe)_5[OH/(Si,Al)_4O_{11}]_2$
Similar Minerals: Augite and tourmaline are distinguished by the difference in cleavage.

Norway 10X

Anatase occurs in Alpine fissures as beautiful crystals. It is especially popular with mineral collectors because of its many varieties of color and form.

Color: Colorless, pink, red, yellow, brown, blue, black. Metallic to adamantine luster.
Cleavage: Usually not visible. Uneven fracture.
Crystal Form: Tetragonal. Acute to flat bipyramids, tabular crystals.
Where Found: In Alpine fissures.

Found with: Rutile, brookite, quartz, feldspar, hematite, apatite.
Hardness: 5½–6
Specific Gravity: 3.8–3.9
Streak Color: White.
Chemical Formula: TiO_2
Similar Minerals: Magnetite has a black streak.

Brookite

Switzerland 10X

Brookite is a relatively rare titanium mineral found in Alpine fissures as beautiful crystals. The tabular crystals from the Alps often display a blackish hourglass-shaped figure in the middle.

Color: Brown, greenish to blackish, usually transparent. Adamantine luster.
Cleavage: Unclear. Uneven fracture.
Crystal Form: Orthorhombic. Thin, tabular crystals, sometimes hexagonal bipyramids.

Where Found: In Alpine fissures.
Found with: Anatase, rutile, titanite, quartz.
Hardness: 5½–6
Specific Gravity: 4.1
Streak Color: White.
Chemical Formula: TiO_2
Similar Minerals: Anatase is clearly tetragonal. Hematite has a different streak.

Leucite

Italy 5X

Leucite is a common mineral in volcanic rocks. Its crystal form —leucitohedral—is so characteristic that it is named for the mineral.

Color: Colorless, white to gray. Vitreous luster.
Cleavage: None. Conchoidal fracture.
Crystal Form: Cubic and tetragonal. Almost exclusively trapezohedral. Developed within lavas.
Where Found: In volcanic rocks.

Found with: Hornblende, augite.
Hardness: 5½–6
Specific Gravity: 2.5
Streak Color: White.
Chemical Formula: $K[AlSi_2O_6]$
Similar Minerals: Analcite practically always occurs as isolated crystals.

West Germany 3X

Augite is a typical mineral of volcanic rocks, in which it can be embedded as crystals about an inch (several centimeters) in size.

Color: Dark green, black. Vitreous luster.
Cleavage: Distinct. The cleavage planes form an angle of about 90 degrees. Conchoidal fracture.
Crystal Form: Monoclinic. Short eight-sided prisms, acicular.
Where Found: In igneous and, especially, volcanic rocks.
Found with: Biotite, olivine, hornblende.
Hardness: 6
Specific Gravity: 3.3–3.5
Streak Color: Greenish.
Chemical Formula: $(Ca,Mg,Fe)_2[(Si,Al)_2O_6]$
Similar Minerals: Hornblende has a different cleavage angle and a different symmetry.

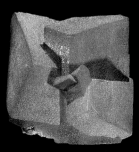

Potassium feldspars are important constituents of many rocks, such as granites, gneisses, or rhyolites. Certain forms, for example amazonite, are also used in making jewelry. The monoclinic, high-temperature forms are known as *orthoclase*. The triclinic, low-temperature forms are called *microcline*; they frequently occur in cavities and geodes of pegmatites, together with quartz and many gem minerals. *Sanidine* is a clear potassium feldspar from volcanic rocks; it and *adularia* are

West Germany 1X *(left)*
Colorado, USA 1X *(top right)*
Switzerland 1X *(bottom left)*

known as Alpine feldspars. *Amazonite* is green potassium feldspar occuring mainly in pegmatites, where it often forms beautiful crystals.

Color: Colorless, white, yellowish, brown, flesh red, emerald green. Vitreous luster.
Cleavage: Easy. Conchoidal fracture.
Crystal Form: Monoclinic and triclinic. Prismatic and tabu-

East Germany 2X

lar crystals, frequently twinned, often massive.

Where Found: In igneous, volcanic, and metamorphic rocks, in pegmatites, Alpine fissures, and hydrothermal veins.

Found with: Quartz, muscovite, plagioclase, biotite, garnet, tourmaline, and others.

Hardness: 6

Specific Gravity: 2.53–2.56

Streak Color: White.

Chemical Formula: $K[AlSi_3O_8]$

Similar Minerals: Quartz has no cleavage. Calcite, barite, and gypsum are softer. Differentiation from plagioclase by simple means is sometimes impossible.

Rutile

Rutile is the most common titanium mineral.

Austria 5X (*top*)
Austria 5X (*bottom*)

Color: Yellowish brown, red, black. Adamantine to metallic luster.
Cleavage: Perfect, but visible only in thick crystals. Conchoidal fracture.
Crystal Form: Tetragonal. Prismatic to acicular crystals. Elbow twins. Repeated twinning produces rings and regular networks (*sagenite*; see photo at top).
Where Found: In pegmatites, Alpine fissures, alluvial deposits.
Found with: Quartz, feldspar, apatite, anatase, brookite.
Hardness: 6
Specific Gravity: 4.2–4.3
Streak Color: Yellowish brown.
Chemical Formula: TiO^2
Similar Minerals: Tourmaline has a different luster. Magnetite has a different streak.

Magnetite is an important and highly valued iron ore with magnetic properties. It is attracted by magnets, turns compass needles, and attracts small particles of iron, such as iron filings.

Switzerland

Color: Iron black. Dull metallic luster.
Cleavage: Scarcely perceptible. Conchoidal fracture.
Crystal Form: Cubic. Octahedral, rhombohedral, often massive.
Where Found: In igneous rocks, contact deposits, crystals in chlorite schists.
Found with: Pyrite, ilmenite, hematite, apatite.
Hardness: 6–6½
Specific Gravity: 5.2
Streak Color: Black.
Chemical Formula: Fe_3O_4
Similar Minerals: Hematite has a red streak.

West Germany 3.5X

Marcasite has the same chemical composition as pyrite but a distinctly different crystal form.

Color: Brass yellow with a tinge of green. Metallic luster.
Cleavage: Poor. Uneven fracture.
Crystal Form: Orthorhombic. Sawtoothed and spear-shaped associated crystals. Often radiated and massive.
Where Found: In hydrothermal veins, clays, and marls.
Found with: Pyrite, pyrrhotite, sphalerite.

Hardness: 6–6½
Specific Gravity: 4.8–4.9
Streak Color: Black.
Chemical Formula: FeS_2
Similar Minerals: Pyrrhotite and arsenopyrite have a different color. Chalcopyrite is softer.

Switzerland 6X

Like orthoclase and microcline, plagioclases belong to the group of feldspars. They are major constituents of many rocks.

Color: Colorless, white, greenish, reddish, gray. Vitreous luster.

Cleavage: Perfect. Conchoidal fracture.

Crystal Form: Triclinic. Prismatic to tabular, often twinned, frequently massive.

Where Found: In igneous, volcanic, and metamorphic rocks; in Alpine fissures.

Found with: Quartz, muscovite, potassium feldspars.

Hardness: 6–6½

Specific Gravity: 2.61–2.77

Streak Color: White.

Chemical Formula: $(Ca,Na)[(Si,Al)_2Si_2O_8]$

Similar Minerals: Quartz has no cleavage. Calcite, barite, and gypsum are softer.

Because of its golden yellow color, pyrite is often confused with gold, which is much softer. For this reason it is commonly called fool's gold.

West Germany 2X (top)
India 6X (bottom)

Color: Bright brass yellow. Metallic luster.

Cleavage: Indistinct. Conchoidal fracture.

Crystal Form: Cubic. Cubes with striated surfaces, pentagonal dodecahedrons (pyritohedrons), and octahedrons are common; often massive.

Where Found: Very widely distributed.

Found with: Hematite, chalcopyrite, galena.

Hardness: 6–6½

Specific Gravity: 5.0–5.2

Streak Color: Black.

Chemical Formula: FeS_2

Similar Minerals: Marcasite is somewhat paler (with a touch of green) and has a different crystal form. Chalcopyrite is much softer. Gold is softer and can be cut.

Switzerland 1X

Hematite is one of the most important iron ores. It can also occur as beautiful crystals.

Color: Red (massive, thin sheets), metallic gray. Metallic luster to dull.
Cleavage: None. Conchoidal fracture.
Crystal Form: Trigonal. Thick and thin sheets, rosettes, radiated with smooth surface, (reniform "kidney ore"; see photo on inside front cover).
Where Found: In metallic ore veins, fissures, and volcanic rocks.
Found with: Pyrite, magnetite.
Hardness: 6½
Specific Gravity: 5.3
Streak Color: Red.
Chemical Formula: Fe_2O_3
Similar Minerals: Cuprite is softer. Magnetite has a black streak.

Epidote is widely distributed in many rocks in the form of minute crystals. In the Alps it forms particularly large, beautiful crystals.

Color: Yellow to black-green. Vitreous luster.
Cleavage: Perfect. Conchoidal fracture.
Crystal Form: Monoclinic. Prismatic, tabular, radiated aggregates.
Where Found: In metamorphic rocks, pegmatites, Alpine fissures.

Austria 4X

Found with: Augite, hornblende, stilbite, apatite.
Hardness: 6–7
Specific Gravity: 3.3–3.5
Streak Color: Gray.
Chemical Formula: $Ca_2[Fe,Al Al_2[O/OH/SiO_4/Si_2O_7]$
Similar Minerals: Hornblende and augite have different cleavages.

Egypt 5X

In addition to being a component of numerous rocks (for example, basalt), olivine is also used in jewelry as a gemstone (peridot).

Color: Yellow-green, bottle green. Vitreous luster.
Cleavage: Poor. Conchoidal fracture.
Crystal Form: Orthorhombic. Prismatic to tabular, often massive.
Where Found: In volcanic and igneous rocks, in marbles.
Found with: Augite, hornblende.
Hardness: 6½–7
Specific Gravity: 3.3
Streak Color: White.
Chemical Formula: $(MgFe)_2[SiO_4]$
Similar Minerals: Apatite is softer and has a different crystal form.

Quebec, Canada 10X

The garnets are a group of widely distributed minerals with the general chemical formula $A_3B_2[SiO_4]_3$, where A is Ca, Mg, Fe, or Mn and B is Fe, Al, Cr, or Ti. Many garnets are used as ornamental stones and gemstones (for example, *pyrope, almandine,* and *demantoid*).

Color: See under **Varieties.** Vitreous luster.

Cleavage: Scarcely visible. Conchoidal fracture.

Crystal Form: Cubic. Most often rhomboidal dodecahedrons and trapezohedrons. Other crystal shapes only secondary and rare. Sometimes also massive.

The Most Common Varieties and Where Found: *Pyrope* (Mg-Al garnet): deep red; found in ultrabasic rocks and serpentinites. *Almandine* (Fe-Al garnet; see photo on p. 55): red-brown; found in gneisses and mica schists. *Spessartine* (Mn-Al garnet): yellow, red-

Austria 3X

brown, black-brown; found in pegmatites and metamorphic rocks. *Grossularite* (Ca-Al garnet; see photo on p. 54): yellow, bright brown, bright green; found in contact rocks. *Andradite* (Ca-Fe garnet): brown, green, black; found in contact rocks, in fissures of serpentinites. Green andradite is also known as *topazolite* and *demantoid*. *Melanite* is a black, Ti-containing andradite. *Uvarovite* (Ca-Cr garnet): emerald green; found in chromium ore deposits.

Hardness: 6½–7½
Specific Gravity: 3.4–4.6
Streak Color: White.
Similar Minerals: Leucite and analcite are softer. Cuprite effervesces in contact with a drop of hydrochloric acid. Magnetite has a more metallic luster than melanite.

Quartz

Quartz is a very common mineral that occurs in numerous colors and forms. It is often used for making jewelry.

Color: Colorless and numerous color varieties (see under **Varieties**). Vitreous to greasy luster.

Cleavage: Scarcely noticeable. Conchoidal fracture.

Crystal Form: Trigonal. High-temperature quartz (formed above 573 °C) is hexagonal. Prismatic. Usually hexagonal in appearance. Trigonal crystals

Peru 2X (left)
Mexico 0.5X (top right)
Switzerland 1X (bottom right)

are formed at lower temperatures. Often massive.

The Most Common Varieties and Where Found:
Rock crystal (p. 56, left): colorless, clear to transparent; found in fissures of gneisses, granites, marbles, and in pegmatite geodes. *Smoky quartz* (p. 56, bottom right): smoke brown to black; found in the same places

East Germany 1X

as rock crystal. *Amethyst* (p. 56, *top right*): violet; found mostly in geodes in lavas and in metallic ore veins. *Rose quartz:* pink; crystals rare, usually massive; found in pegmatites. *Jasper:* colored red by hematite inclusions; found in ore veins and in clays. *Chalcedony:* reniform crusts lining cavities in lavas and in ore veins, also in sedimentary rocks. Colors are widely varied: red to red-brown (*carnelian*), green (*chrysoprase*), blue; *agate* displays concentric layers of various colors (p. 57). *Flint, firestone:* gray to brown-colored nodules in limestones.

Hardness: 7
Specific Gravity: 2.65
Streak Color: White.
Chemical Formula: SiO_2
Similar Minerals: Hardness and resistance to acid differentiate quartz from other common minerals.

Brazil 1X

Tourmalines occur in various colors. The transparent specimens are valuable gemstones.

Color: Colorless, green, yellow, pink, red, blue, brown, black (schorl). Vitreous luster.
Cleavage: None. Conchoidal fracture.
Crystal Form: Trigonal. Prismatic crystals, triangular in cross section.
Where Found: In pegmatites, metamorphic rocks.
Found with: Potassium feldspars, quartz, muscovite.

Hardness: 7
Specific Gravity: 3.0–3.25
Streak Color: White.
Chemical Formula: $(Na,Li)(Fe,Mn,Mg)_3Al_6[(OH)_4/(BO_3)_3/Si_6O_{18}]$
Similar Minerals: Augite and hornblende have typical cleavages. Epidote and beryl have different crystal forms.

Beryl is a valuable gemstone, especially in its aquamarine and emerald color varieties.

Pakistan 2X (*top left*)
Utah, USA 4X (*top right*)
Colombia 3X (*bottom*)

Color: Colorless, yellow, blue (*aquamarine;* photo at top left), pink (*morganite;* photo at top right), red, green (*emerald;* photo at bottom). Vitreous luster.

Cleavage: Basal, sometimes perceptible. Conchoidal fracture.

Crystal Form: Hexagonal. Prismatic crystals, embedded and free.

Where Found: In pegmatites.
Found with: Quartz, feldspar.
Hardness: 7½–8
Specific Gravity: 2.63–2.80
Streak Color: White.
Chemical Formula: $Al_2Be_3[Si_6O_{18}]$
Similar Minerals: Apatite is softer. Topaz, tourmaline, and quartz have different crystal forms.

East Germany 5X

Topaz occurs in many color varieties, all of which are prized as valuable gemstones.

Color: Colorless, white, yellow, blue, green, red, violet. Vitreous luster.
Cleavage: Perfect. Conchoidal fracture.
Crystal Form: Orthorhombic. Short or long prismatic crystals, also embedded in rocks.
Where Found: In pegmatites, pneumatolytic deposits, alluvial deposits.
Found with: Muscovite, fluorite, quartz, tourmaline, feldspar.
Hardness: 8
Specific Gravity: 3.5–3.6
Streak Color: White.
Chemical Formula: $Al_2[F_2/SiO_4]$
Similar Minerals: Quartz is lighter and has no cleavage. Fluorite is softer.

India 4X

Red (*ruby*) and blue (*sapphire*) color varieties of corundum are valuable gemstones and, therefore, are produced artificially in large quantities.

Color: Blue (*sapphire*), red (*ruby*), yellow, green, brown, violet, colorless. Vitreous luster.
Cleavage: Poor. Conchoidal fracture.
Crystal Form: Trigonal. Prismatic, bipyramidal, and tabular crystals.
Where Found: In pegmatites, amphibolites, marbles, alluvial deposits.
Found with: Magnetite, spinel, calcite, diaspore.
Hardness: 9
Specific Gravity: 3.9–4.1
Streak Color: White.
Chemical Formula: Al_2O_3
Similar Minerals: Hardness and specific gravity make corundum unmistakable.

South Africa 4X

Diamonds are the hardest minerals and the most valuable gemstones. Because of their hardness, industrial quality diamonds are used for files, drill bits, and grinding wheels.

Color: Colorless, yellow, brown, reddish, greenish, blue, gray. Adamantine luster.
Cleavage: Perfect octahedral. Conchoidal fracture.
Crystal Form: Cubic. Most often octahedral.
Where Found: In basic igneous rocks; also in alluvial deposits.
Found with: Olivine, phlogopite, garnet.
Hardness: 10
Specific Gravity: 3.52
Streak Color: White.
Chemical Formula: C
Similar Minerals: Hardness differentiates diamonds from all other minerals.

Minerals Index

The Author
Rupert Hochleitner is a professional mineralogist at the Institute
for Crystallography and Mineralogy in Munich and lecturer in
mineralogy at the Munich Adult Education Program. He is editor
in chief of the mineralogy journal *Lapis* and author of Barron's
Gemstones.

English translation © Copyright 1990
by Barron's Educational Series, Inc.

© Copyright 1988 by Gräfe and Unzer
GmbH, Munich, West Germany
The title of the German book is *Mineralien*

Translated from the German by Elizabeth D. Crawford
Consulting Editor: Albert Carozzi, Ph.D.

All rights reserved.
No part of this book may be reproduced in any form,
by photostat, microfilm, xerography, or any other
means, or incorporated into any information retrieval
system, electronic or mechanical, without the written
permission of the copyright owner.

All inquiries should be addressed to:
Barron's Educational Series, Inc.
250 Wireless Boulevard
Hauppauge, NY 11788

International Standard Book No. 0-8120-4456-8

Library of Congress Catalog Card No. 90-245

Hochleitner, Rupert.
   [Mineralien. English]
   Minerals / Rupert Hochleitner; [translated
from the German by Elizabeth D. Crawford].
      64 p.   cm.
   Translation of: Mineralien.
   ISBN (invalid) 0-8120-4456-8
   1. Mineralogy.   I. Title.
QE372.2.H6313   1990
549—dc20   90-245
                                           CIP

PRINTED IN HONG KONG

9012 9927 987654321

Photographers: Huber: 5, 35; Medenbach:
48; Offermann: 8 right, inside front cover
(1). All others by Hochleitner.